Great National Soccer Teams / Grandes selecciones del fútbol mundial

ARGENTINA

José María Obregón

English translation: Megan Benson

PowerKiDS press

Editorial Buenas Letras™
New York

Published in 2010 by The Rosen Publishing Group, Inc.
29 East 21st Street, New York, NY 10010

First Edition

Editor: Nicole Pristash
Book Design: Julio Gil
Photo Researcher: Jessica Gerweck

Photo Credits: Cover Mark Dadswell/Getty Images; back cover, p. 13 Bob Thomas/Getty Images; p. 5 Getty Images; p. 7 Pedro Ugarte/AFP/Getty Images; p. 9 Christof Koepsel/Bongarts/Getty Images; p. 11 Rodrigo Arangua/AFP/Getty Images; p. 15 Allsport UK/Allsport/Getty Images; p. 17 Chris Cole/Allsport/Getty Images; p. 19 Koji Watanabe/Getty Images; p. 21 (flag) Shutterstock.com; p. 21 (left) Jack Guez/AFP/Getty Images; p. 21 (middle) Ross Kinnaird/Getty Images.

Library of Congress Cataloging-in-Publication Data

Obregón, José María, 1963–
   Argentina / José María Obregón. — 1st ed.
      p. cm. — (Great national soccer teams = Grandes selecciones nacionales de fútbol)
   Includes index.
   ISBN 978-1-4042-8088-5 (library binding) — ISBN 978-1-4358-2495-9 (pbk.) —
ISBN 978-1-4358-2496-6 (6-pack)
   1. Soccer—Argentina—Juvenile literature. 2. Soccer teams—Argentina—Juvenile literature. I. Title.
   GV944.A7O37 2010
   796.3340982—dc22
                                    2008054946

Manufactured in the United States of America

CONTENTS

CONTENIDO

One of the most successful soccer teams in the world is the Argentinean national team. It has won more international **tournaments** than any other national team. Argentina has won the FIFA U-20 **World Cup** 6 times, the Copa América 14 times, and the World Cup twice.

La selección de Argentina es el equipo de fútbol con más **torneos** ganados a nivel internacional. Argentina ha ganado 6 veces la **Copa del Mundo** FIFA Sub-20, 14 veces la Copa América y 2 veces la Copa del Mundo.

Argentinean player Mario Kempes (center) cheers after scoring a goal during the 1978 World Cup final.

El jugador Mario Kempes (al centro) celebra su gol durante la final de la Copa del Mundo de 1978.

5

The Argentinean national team has had many talented players throughout its history. Players Diego Armando Maradona, Mario Kempes, Diego Simeone, Gabriel Batistuta, and Lionel Messi have helped the team reach a level of greatness in the soccer world and among the team's fans.

La selección de Argentina ha contado en su historia con jugadores de gran talento. Jugadores como Diego Armando Maradona, Mario Kempes, Diego Simeone, Gabriel Batistuta y Lionel Messi le han dado a Argentina mucho prestigio a nivel mundial y entre sus seguidores.

Here Lionel Messi (right) is shown playing in the 2008 Olympic soccer final game against Nigeria.

Lionel Messi (derecha) durante la final de fútbol de los Juegos Olímpicos 2008 contra Nigeria.

Soccer is a very important sport in Argentina. Argentinean fans get very excited about the game, and they love their national team. Fans call the team the *Albiceleste* because of the team's colors, which are white and light blue. "Albiceleste" means "white and light blue" in Spanish.

El fútbol es muy importante en Argentina y se vive con mucha pasión. Los aficionados argentinos apoyan con todo a su selección, a la que llaman la Albiceleste por los colores blanco y azul celeste de la bandera argentina y su uniforme.

This Argentinean fan is proudly wearing the colors of the Albiceleste.

Una aficionada argentina muestra con orgullo los colores de la Albiceleste.

9

The Argentinean team's playing style is based on the players' strength and skill. The team's players are very smart, and they know just what to do on the field. The players have a lot of willpower, too. They put a lot of much-needed energy, or power, into their games.

El estilo del fútbol argentino se basa en la fuerza y la habilidad de sus jugadores. Los albicelestes son muy inteligentes para jugar y saben muy bien qué hacer en el campo de juego. Además, los argentinos ponen mucha voluntad en todos sus partidos.

In 1930, Argentina played in the very first World Cup, but it lost the final game. In 1978, 48 years later, the Albiceleste won its first World Cup. Playing at home, the Argentineans beat the Dutch. Player Mario Kempes scored two goals in the final game.

En 1930, Argentina perdió la final de la primera Copa del Mundo. Cuarenta y ocho años más tarde, la Albiceleste ganó su primera Copa del Mundo en 1978. Jugando en casa, los argentinos derrotaron a Holanda en la final con dos goles de Mario Kempes.

Here you can see the team captain, Daniel Passarella, raising the trophy at the 1978 World Cup.

Aquí vemos al capitán Daniel Passarella levantar el trofeo en la Copa del Mundo 1978.

Argentina won its second World Cup in Mexico, in 1986. The star of the tournament was Diego Armando Maradona. Maradona scored five goals, including the so-called Goal of the Century. Maradona **dribbled** past five players and the goalie before kicking the ball into the net!

Argentina ganó su segunda Copa del Mundo en México 1986. Diego Armando Maradona fue la estrella de esta copa. Maradona anotó cinco goles, incluyendo el llamado Gol del Siglo. ¡En este gol, Maradona **burló** a cinco jugadores y al portero del equipo contrario antes de poner el balón en las redes!

Maradona (center) makes his move among British players in what will become the Goal of the Century.

Maradona (al centro) comienza su gambeta entre los jugadores de Inglaterra en el Gol del Siglo.

15

Maradona scored close to 350 goals in his career. He was also a great team player, helping his teammates score many goals, too. In 2000, FIFA named Maradona the best soccer player of the century. FIFA is the International Federation of Association Football.

Maradona anotó cerca de 350 goles en su carrera. Pero, además, Maradona trabajaba muy bien en equipo, ayudando a que sus compañeros anotaran muchos goles. En 2000, FIFA nombró a Maradona el mejor jugador de fútbol de la historia. FIFA es la Federación Internacional de Fútbol.

Many people say Maradona's skills were so great that he is among the best players in history.

Muchos piensan que la habilidad de Maradona lo hace uno de los mejores jugadores en la historia.

17

In recent years, Argentina has been very successful in the **Olympic Games**. The Albiceleste won the gold medal in Athens 2004 and Beijing 2008. Argentinean **striker** Carlos Tévez was named the best scorer of the games in 2004 after scoring eight goals.

En los años recientes Argentina ha tenido mucho éxito en los **Juegos Olímpicos**. La Albiceleste ganó la medalla de oro en Atenas 2004 y Pekín 2008. El **delantero** argentino, Carlos Tévez, fue el máximo goleador del torneo de 2004 con 8 goles.

Aquí vemos a los jugadores argentinos celebrando su segunda medalla de oro en el fútbol olímpico.

It is said that Argentina is a factory for the best players. Today, young stars like Fernando Gago, Ángel di María, Sergio Kun Agüero, and Lionel Messi are helping prove that Argentina will continue to be one of the best soccer teams in the world.

Se dice que Argentina es una fábrica de grandes jugadores. Hoy, las jóvenes estrellas de la Albiceleste como Fernando Gago, Ángel di María, Sergio Kun Agüero y Lionel Messi garantizan que Argentina seguirá siendo una de las mejores selecciones del mundo.

ARGENTINA

Argentinean Football Confederation
Year Founded: 1893

Asociación del Fútbol Argentino
Año de fundación: 1893

Home
Local

Away
Visitante

Player Highlights / Jugadores destacados

Most Caps */ Más convocatorias

Javier Zanetti (1994–)
128 caps / 128 convocatorias

* Appearances with the national soccer team

Top Scorer / Mejor anotador

Gabriel Batistuta (1991–2002)
56 goals / 56 goles

Top Player / Mejor jugador

Diego Armando Maradona (1977–1994)
Winner of the World Cup 1986 and
FIFA best football player of the century
/ Ganador de la Copa del Mundo 1986
/ Mejor jugador FIFA del siglo

Team Highlights / Palmarés del equipo

FIFA World Cup™/ Copa Mundial FIFA
Appearances / Participaciones: 14
Winner / Ganador: 1978, 1986
Runner-Up / Segundo: 1930, 1990

Copa América
Winner / Ganador: 1921, 1925, 1927,
1929, 1937, 1941, 1945, 1946, 1947,
1955, 1957, 1959, 1991, 1993

FIFA Confederations Cup /
Copa Confederaciones FIFA
Winner / Ganador: 1992

FIFA U-20 World Cup / Copa Mundial FIFA Sub-20
Winner / Ganador: 1979, 1995, 1997, 2001,
2005, 2007

Olympics / Olimpíadas
Winner / Ganador: 2004, 2008

21

GLOSSARY / GLOSARIO

dribbled (DRIH-beld) Kicked the ball while running.

Olympic Games (uh-LIM-pik GAYMZ) When the best sports players in the world meet every four years to play against each other.

striker (STRY-ker) A player who scores goals.

tournaments (TOR-nuh-ments) Groups of games that decide the best team.

World Cup (WUR-uld KUP) A group of games that takes place every four years with teams from around the world.

---

burlar Mover el balón entre los jugadores contrarios.

Copa del Mundo (la) Competencia de fútbol, cada 4 años, en la que juegan los mejores equipos del mundo.

delantero (el) Un jugador que anota goles.

Juegos Olímpicos (los) Competición deportiva mundial que se realiza cada cuatro años.

torneos (los) Grupos de partidos que deciden cuál es el mejor equipo.

RESOURCES / RECURSOS

Books in English / Libros en inglés

Crawford, Andy. *Soccer*. New York: DK Publishing, 2005.

Minden, Cecilia. *Soccer*. Ann Arbor, MI: Cherry Lake Publishing, 2009.

Books in Spanish / Libros en español

Dann, Sarah. *Fútbol en acción (Soccer in Action)*. New York: Crabtree Publishing, 2005.

Obregón, José María. *Lionel Messi*. New York: PowerKids Press/Editorial Buenas Letras, 2009.

Web Sites

Due to the changing nature of Internet links, PowerKids Press has developed an online list of Web sites related to the subject of this book. This site is updated regularly. Please use this link to access the list:
www.powerkidslinks.com/soct/argentina/

INDEX

ÍNDICE